LIVE

NO

LIES

Recognize and Resist the Three
Enemies That Sabotage Your Peace

Study Guide | Four Sessions

John Mark Comer

HarperChristian
Resources

Live No Lies Study Guide
© 2021 by John Mark Comer

Requests for information should be addressed to:
HarperChristian Resources, 3900 Sparks Dr. SE, Grand Rapids, Michigan 49546

ISBN 978-0-310-14327-7 (softcover)

ISBN 978-0-310-14328-4 (ebook)

HarperChristian Resources titles may be purchased in bulk for church, business, fundraising, or ministry use. For information, please e-mail ResourceSpecialist@ChurchSource.com.

First Printing December 2021 / Printed in the United States of America
23 24 25 26 27 LBC 7 6 5 4 3

CONTENTS

INTRODUCTION

Life is a struggle. Whether you consider that an obvious understatement or an exaggerated generalization, the statement still reflects what is true. No matter how much you earn, achieve, accomplish, or create, you are not immune to cancer, divorce, car trouble, gossip, theft, bankruptcy, and betrayal. You might insulate yourself for a short while, but ultimately trouble catches up to you one way or another. Sometimes, it never seems to let go.

Jesus knew the ways of this world. He said as much during his ministry on earth: "In this world you will have trouble" (John 16:33). This is not a pessimistic expectation or a likely possibility. It's an observation of *reality*. Once we're born into this world, we will experience trouble consistently throughout our lives.

Nevertheless, Jesus, along with various writers in the Bible's New Testament, command us to rejoice and choose to be joyful regardless of our circumstances. So, the situation is clear: we will have trouble, but we can choose joy. But how, let alone why, can we choose joy in the midst of losing a loved one, losing a job, watching a child hurt, or seeing a business go under?

This dilemma manifests itself in the tension between pain and suffering. Pain is what happens. Suffering is how we feel about what happens and the meaning, if any, that we make from it. Pain is inevitable, but apparently suffering reflects the choices we make, which usually result from the beliefs we hold. And the beliefs we hold are not always true.

In fact, for many of us, most of what we believe is not true. Lies have infiltrated our thinking, our perceptions, our attitudes, and our actions. The problem isn't so much that we *tell* lies but that we *live* them. We let them into our bodies, minds, and hearts—and they sabotage our peace and wreak havoc on our physical, emotional, and spiritual health.

You are actually in the middle of a war between lies and truth. This may sound harsh or militaristic, but your choice is not whether to fight or abstain from battle. Your choice is whether to win or to surrender: to build your life on lies and deception or to make truth your foundation.

Ancient followers of Jesus experienced this war and developed a paradigm for how to win it. They described three primary enemies of the soul: the devil, the flesh, and the world. The *Live No Lies* study will draw from this ancient wisdom gleaned from past saints and help you see how each of these three enemies manifest in our modern era—and how you can combat them. After all, you have to recognize the lies each of these foes perpetuates before you can resist them.

This study guide complements the message of hope in *Live No Lies* and will help you apply it directly to your life. Each session looks at specific ways lies infiltrate your life and how you can eradicate them with the living truth of God's Word. Together, they will help you win the war so that the truth does indeed set you free from the lies that have been holding you back.

HOW TO USE THIS GUIDE

STRUCTURE OF THE STUDY

The *Live No Lies* video study is designed to be experienced in a group setting (such as a Bible study, Sunday school class, or other small-group gathering) and also as an individual study. Each session begins with a welcome section, two questions to get you thinking about the topic, and a reading from the Bible. You will then watch a video with John Mark Comer, which can be accessed via the streaming code found on the inside front cover. If you are doing the study with a group, you will then engage in some directed discussion. If the gathering is large, your leader may split everyone into smaller groups of five or six people to make sure everyone has enough time to participate in discussions.

MATERIALS NEEDED

Everyone in your group will need his or her own copy of this study guide, which includes the opening questions you will discuss, notes for video segments, directions for activities and discussion questions, and personal studies in between sessions. You may also want a copy of the book *Live No*

Lies, which provides further insights into the material you are covering in this study. To aid your study experience, you will be encouraged to make sure you've read specific chapters in the book to prepare for the group's next meeting.

FACILITATION

Your group will need to appoint a person to serve as a facilitator. This person will be responsible for starting the video and keeping track of time during discussions and activities. Facilitators may also read questions aloud and monitor discussions, prompting participants to respond and assuring that everyone has the opportunity to participate. If you have been chosen for this role, note there are additional instructions and resources in the back of this guide to help you lead your group members through the study.

PERSONAL STUDIES

During the week, you can maximize the impact of the course with the personal studies provided for each session. You can treat each personal study section like a devotional and use them in whatever way works best for your schedule. You could do one section each day for three days of the week or complete them all in one sitting. These personal studies are not intended to be burdensome or time-consuming but to provide a richer experience and continuity in between your group sessions.

THE STRUGGLE IS REAL

Fight the good fight of the faith.
1 TIMOTHY 6:12

WELCOME

What comes to your mind when you think of the Christian life? Perhaps you picture going to church with your family on Sundays. Or maybe the first image that appears is spending time in the Bible and in prayer with God. Or it might be that you envision serving others and helping those in need. All of these are aspects of the Christian life. But it's likely that what you don't picture are soldiers on a battlefield waging a war against a powerful enemy.

Many of us today are actually uncomfortable with viewing spirituality as a struggle or using any type of military metaphor to describe our journey of faith. But the writers of the New Testament had no such qualms. Again and again, we find them associating the act of following Christ to a kind of war for our soul. We see this particularly in the writings of the apostle Paul, who warned one group of believers that their struggle was "not against flesh and blood, but against . . . the spiritual forces of evil" (Ephesians 6:12). He urged them to "suit up" for the fight by putting on the armor of God so they could demolish the strongholds of evil.

We find similar imagery used throughout the history of the Christian church. Many of the early saints saw the Christian life as nothing less than a battle against three forces of the devil, the flesh, and the world. While we may be tempted to roll our eyes at such an idea, the reality is that these three enemies are still at work today to not just *disrupt* our lives but to actually *destroy* us. As Jesus said, "The devil . . . was a murderer from the beginning" (John 8:44).

While it's fine for us to be skeptical, uncertain, or even uneasy about viewing ourselves as fighters for the faith, we dare not dismiss the reality of this truth. So, in this first session, we will begin by learning how to recognize these enemies and their assaults. As we do, we can be assured that God does not leave us defenseless against these foes. We have been given the power to defeat them! By following the example that Christ has set for us, and by learning from his teachings, we can experience peace and overcome any force that comes against us.

SHARE

If you or your group members are just getting to know one another, take a few minutes to introduce yourselves. Then, to get things started, discuss one of the following questions:

- Do you consider yourself more of a peacemaker or someone who doesn't mind jumping into the fray at home or at work? How do you typically respond?

— *or* —

- What usually comes to mind when you hear combat language applied to faith and spirituality? Why do you suppose you have those associations?

READ

Invite someone to read aloud the following passage. Listen for fresh insights as you hear the verse being read and then discuss the questions that follow.

Finally, be strong in the Lord and in his mighty power. Put on the full armor of God, so that you can take your stand against the devil's schemes. For our struggle is not against flesh and blood, but against the rulers, against the authorities, against the powers of this dark world and against the spiritual forces of evil in the heavenly realms. Therefore put on the full armor of God, so that when the day of evil comes, you may be able to stand your ground, and after you have done everything, to stand. Stand firm then, with the belt of truth buckled around your waist, with the breastplate of righteousness in place, and with your feet fitted with the readiness that comes from the gospel of peace. In addition to all this, take up the shield of faith, with which you can extinguish all the flaming arrows of the evil one. Take the helmet of salvation and the sword of the Spirit, which is the word of God. And pray in the Spirit on all occasions with all kinds of prayers and requests. With this in mind, be alert and always keep on praying for all the Lord's people.

Ephesians 6:10–18

What image or description stands out to you in this passage? Why do you think it resonates with you so much right now?

Do you agree that your greatest struggles are spiritual and not material? Why or why not?

WATCH

Play the video segment for session one (see the streaming video access provided on the inside front cover). As you watch, use the following outline to record any thoughts or concepts that stand out to you.

Life, as good and rich as it is, is full of suffering and pain. No life is up and to the right nonstop. At times, it is just a struggle to keep on.

Pain is what is—the death of a loved one, a diagnosis, a divorce, a failure, a betrayal we just can't shake. *Suffering* is how we feel about what is and the meaning we make, or we don't make, from going through our pain.

The New Testament authors did not fear using military metaphors. They likened following Jesus not only to a struggle but also to a kind of war for the soul.

The early church fathers and mothers viewed the story of Jesus' temptation in the wilderness in a different way than we would expect. They saw it as the devil speaking a lie over Jesus—and Jesus refusing to listen to or believe that lie.

Evagrius Ponticus, a desert father, said our struggle in spirituality and in life, as a whole, is with three basic enemies:

1. Our thoughts (the devil)

2. Our passions (the flesh)

3. Our world itself

Followers of Jesus are at war with the world, and the flesh, and the devil. These three enemies use *deceptive ideas* (the devil), that play to *disordered desires* (the flesh), that are normalized in a *sinful society* (the world).

DISCUSS

As you consider what you just watched, use the following questions to discuss these ideas, their basis in Scripture, and their application in your life with your group members.

1 What stands out in the video teaching that seems especially true right now in your life? How do you see this truth manifesting itself in your present circumstances?

2 What do you struggle to accept or outright reject in the teaching you just watched? Why? What prevents you from agreeing with this point?

3 How do you feel about being a spiritual warrior who is up against these three enemies of your soul—the devil, the flesh, the world? On a scale of 1 to 10, with 1 being "very skeptical" and 10 being "very certain," what score reflects your level of certainty about the existence of these enemies in your life today?

4 In our world today as you see it, what are some specific struggles that result from the attacks of the devil? From the flesh? From the world?

5 Which of these three enemies troubles you the most right now? When and where do you struggle the most to follow Jesus, love others, and maintain faith in God?

6 When have you experienced a spiritual attack that you recognized as an enemy assault? How did you handle that situation at the time? What did you learn from it?

LEARN

Refusing to live the lies perpetuated by your enemies requires deliberate attention, strong convictions, and mindful awareness of spiritual truth. In this first session, you've started the process of exploring what it means to recognize these enemies in order to defeat them. As you reflect on the group discussion and what you will take away from this session, consider how you can remain open to new ways of thinking about spiritual battles and spiritual defense tactics.

Toward the end of each session, you will find an exercise designed to help you remain open to the teaching and to grow stronger in your faith as you reclaim your peace. This practice is also a way to help others in your group as you learn and grow together. For this first session, look at the passage you read aloud earlier, Ephesians 6:10–18. Think about each piece of spiritual armor and its purpose in battle against the powers of darkness. Next, with this list in mind, consider your own spiritual arsenal and where you feel most vulnerable or weak right now.

Finally, think about your expectations for this group study and what you desire most in your relationship with the Lord. Consider what it means for you to identify the lies in your life right now and refute them with eternal truth. Try to identify what you need most in your life presently in order to see the lies, overcome the enemies, and enjoy intimacy with God.

PRAY

Conclude your session by sharing any requests you would like the group to lift up in prayer. Thank God for bringing you together for this study so that you can help and encourage one another as you seek to recognize your spiritual enemies and to resist their attacks on your soul. Ask God for protection against any of the enemy's tricks and lies as you complete this group study. Trust God to give you eyes to see and ears to hear the truth of his Word.

PERSONAL STUDY

Take some time to review the material you've covered this week by engaging in any or all of the following between-sessions activities. In each study, you will first take a moment to **reflect** on what you've learned during the group time and consider the takeaways. You will then seek to **recognize** the truth and **resist** the lies of your enemies by studying a passage from God's Word. Finally, you will explore some truths on how to **rejoice** as you apply these biblical concepts to your own life. For this opening week, you may want to first review the introductory material in *Live No Lies*, including "The War on Lies" and "A Manifesto for Exile." The time you invest will be well spent, so let God use it to draw you closer to him. At the start of the next session, you will have a few minutes to share any insights that you learned with the group.

REFLECT

By beginning this study, you have embarked on a journey of exploration—one that requires you to reconsider what you believe and why you believe those things. It can be hard to see clearly and objectively when many of these assumptions have been accepted for years. But reclaiming your life and experiencing true peace is at stake—and more than worth the effort.

Lies are the ammunition of your spiritual enemies, and the best lies often incorporate elements of truth, sometimes making them even more difficult to discern. So, as you begin recognizing the false beliefs and inaccurate assumptions that have infiltrated your thinking, it's important to trust God to reveal his truth.

We see this kind of faith in God expressed in Psalm 23, one of the best-known and most-beloved passages from Scripture. Read through these verses, opening your heart and mind to God, and seeking his guidance and wisdom as you read. Then answer the questions that follow to help you prepare for any spiritual struggles that you may encounter during this study.

> The LORD is my shepherd, I lack nothing.
>> He makes me lie down in green pastures,
> he leads me beside quiet waters,
>> he refreshes my soul.
> He guides me along the right paths
>> for his name's sake.
> Even though I walk
>> through the darkest valley,
> I will fear no evil,
>> for you are with me;
> your rod and your staff,

they comfort me.
You prepare a table before me
in the presence of my enemies.

Psalm 23:1–5

What three words would you use to describe your relationship with God right now? How do they reflect your view of him? How do they express the way you see yourself?

When have you experienced God's presence in your life during trials or times of strife? How did he comfort and provide for you, much like the Good Shepherd in the psalm, even in the midst of tough times?

How do you feel knowing that examining your life for the lies you believe may potentially change your view of reality? What do you fear most? Why?

RECOGNIZE AND RESIST

For many of the ancient saints of the Christian faith, the encounter Jesus had with the devil, after fasting and praying alone for forty days in the desert, illustrates how we can combat the lies the enemy uses to tempt us with as well. The way they viewed this spiritual showdown differs from how we tend to interpret it initially today. They zeroed in on the way the devil speaks lies over Jesus, attempting to seduce Him into the selfishness of sin, and the way Jesus refuses to consider these lies from the enemy. Instead of arguing or debating, Jesus focuses his thoughts on the corresponding truth from the ancient scriptures. In repeating truth to His attacker, Jesus kept His consciousness tethered to truth, leaving no room for the subtle art of subterfuge from Satan.

Past followers of Jesus have practiced this same kind of mindfulness laser-focused on the truth of God's Word. They realized that it wasn't enough to recognize or refute the devil, but that Jesus made sure to bring truth front-and-center. This practice became the essence of their spiritual battle strategy, one that we can emulate as we discern truth from our enemy's lies. Read through the passage below and then answer the questions that follow.

> Then Jesus was led by the Spirit into the wilderness to be tempted by the devil. After fasting forty days and forty nights, he was hungry. The tempter came to him and said, "If you are the Son of God, tell these stones to become bread."

Jesus answered, "It is written: 'Man shall not live on bread alone, but on every word that comes from the mouth of God.'"

Then the devil took him to the holy city and had him stand on the highest point of the temple. "If you are the Son of God," he said, "throw yourself down. For it is written:

"'He will command his angels concerning you,
and they will lift you up in their hands,
so that you will not strike your foot against a stone.'"

Jesus answered him, "It is also written: 'Do not put the Lord your God to the test.'"

Again, the devil took him to a very high mountain and showed him all the kingdoms of the world and their splendor. "All this I will give you," he said, "if you will bow down and worship me."

Jesus said to him, "Away from me, Satan! For it is written: 'Worship the Lord your God, and serve him only.'"

Then the devil left him, and angels came and attended him.

Matthew 4:1–11

Which word or phrase resonates the most with you in this passage? Why do you think it is especially significant to you at this time?

How does each of the devil's temptations play on a perceived need or physical weakness of Jesus? When has the enemy tried to tempt you during a vulnerable or weak moment?

Notice how the devil ties his lies onto truths using the construction of "if . . . then." How does this strategy make it more difficult for us to see truth clearly?

The devil attacks Jesus in three key areas: appetites, identity, and idolatry. Satan knows Jesus is hungry after fasting for forty days, knows he might be apprehensive now that he is about to begin his public ministry, and knows that his reliance on the Father's power has not yet been tested. What lie does the devil try to use over Jesus in each instance? How does the corresponding truth that Jesus speaks explode the lie?

How have you been tempted in one or all of these three areas recently? How did you respond at the time? How would you respond differently now?

What would be required for you to respond like Jesus when you encounter temptations designed to target your weaknesses? What do you need to do right now in order to strengthen your defenses?

REJOICE

The apostle Paul instructed, "Give thanks in all circumstances; for this is God's will for you in Christ Jesus" (1 Thessalonians 5:18). Notice he didn't say to give thanks when things are going well or when you feel especially content. No, you are to give thanks in *all* circumstances. So, no matter how you feel or what your circumstances might be at present, list ten things—big or small or in-between—that you are thankful for at this moment.

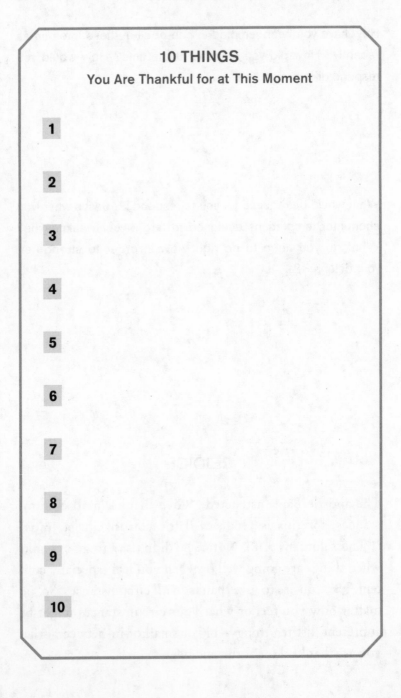

10 THINGS
You Are Thankful for at This Moment

1

2

3

4

5

6

7

8

9

10

After you've finished, read over your list and spend a few moments thanking God for the ways he has blessed you and continues to bless you. Considering this list (or part of it) with your group members at your next session, along with any other ideas resulting from this study or your reflection of the group's first meeting. Use the following questions to help you process your response as you decide what, if anything, you would like to share.

What was your biggest takeaway from your group's first meeting?

What did you enjoy most about your time in the group? What would you change or want to do differently at the next meeting?

How has your perspective on spiritual struggles changed since starting this study? What has stood out or surprised you the most?

For Next Week: Before your group's next session, read chapters 1–4 in *Live No Lies*.

THE TRUTH
ABOUT LIES

The truth will set you free.

JOHN 8:32

WELCOME

In our modern age, it is common for people to dismiss the devil as being just a myth or superstition that spawned in a pre-scientific age. But the Bible is clear that the devil is a *real* entity who has a *real* desire to kill and destroy us. We find him as far back as the Garden of Eden, where he is seeking to undermine God's creation by deceiving the first humans.

When we come to the New Testament, we see Jesus referring to the devil as a real entity and primary source of evil in this world. We find him pointing out the devil's real presence on this earth in a direct and practical way—by calling out the people he encountered who were following the enemy and conversing in his native language of lies. In fact, Jesus recognized humanity's primary war against the devil as a fight to believe truth over lies.

Today, we often fall into one of two camps when it comes to the devil. On the one hand, we dismiss him as just a cosmic spoiler of the goodness of God. On the other hand, we see him in every circumstance and fear his influence. Both extremes lead to an inaccurate assessment of our enemy and the strategies he employs against us. Both cause us to miss that his primary weapon is to distort reality so that he can convince us that his lies are the truth.

As we will discuss in this session, understanding what is *true* and what is *false* is critical in our lives. When we believe *truth*—ideas that correspond to reality as expressed in God's Word—we show up to the world in a way that causes us to flourish and thrive. But when we believe *lies*—ideas that do not correspond to the reality found in God's Word—we show up in a way that causes us to struggle to thrive. Jesus invites us to know the truth and be set free by it. His invitation requires us to rethink what we assume is true and put our trust in him.

SHARE

If you or any of your group members are just getting to know one another, take a few minutes to introduce yourselves and share any insights you have from last week's personal study. Then, to get things started, discuss one of the following questions:

- What are some of the ways that the devil is characterized in our world today? How do people tend to downplay and dismiss his influence?

— *or* —

- How do you discern between what is true and what is false? What criteria do you use to make your decision?

READ

Invite someone to read aloud the following passage. Listen for fresh insights as you hear the verse being read and then discuss the questions that follow.

> Jesus said to them, "If God were your Father, you would love me, for I have come here from God. I have not come on my own; God sent me. Why is my language not clear to you? Because you are unable to hear what I say. You belong to your father, the devil, and you want to carry out your father's desires. He was a murderer from the beginning, not holding to the truth, for there is no truth in him. When he lies, he speaks his native language, for he is a liar and the father of lies. Yet because I tell the truth, you do not believe me! Can any of you prove me guilty of sin? If I am telling the truth, why don't you believe me? Whoever belongs to God hears what God says. The reason you do not hear is that you do not belong to God."
>
> *John 8:42–47*

Jesus was speaking to the Jewish religious leaders of his day. Why do you suppose they refused to accept him as God's Son, the Messiah?

What is the logic informing Jesus' condemnation of these leaders? What surprises you most in what Jesus has to say to them?

WATCH

Play the video segment for session two (see the streaming video access provided on the inside front cover). As you watch, use the following outline to record any thoughts or concepts that stand out to you.

Jesus gave this rebuke to the Pharisees: "You belong to your father, the devil, and you want to carry out your father's desires. He was a murderer from the beginning, not holding to the truth, for there is no truth in him. When he lies, he speaks his native language, for he is a liar and the father of lies" (John 8:44). Notice that Jesus recognized the following:

1. There is a devil.

2. The devil's end goal is to spread death.

3. The devil's means are lies.

Whenever people blame the devil for silly things, it makes it hard not just to write the devil off entirely and throw the baby out with the bath water. But the danger for most of us is not that we see a demon behind every single bush. It's more likely that we just ignore him entirely.

Jesus sees our primary war against the devil as a fight to believe truth over lies. The simplest definition of truth is reality—meaning that which corresponds to reality. Truth is what we can rely on as real.

We all live from what psychologists call mental maps—reference points by which we navigate the world. If our mental maps are not true, we end up lost in the dystopian wasteland of bad cell coverage and glitchy Google Maps.

When we believe truth (ideas that correspond to reality), we show up to reality and live in such a way that we flourish and thrive. When we believe lies (ideas not congruent with the reality of God's design), we allow the cancer of those lies to infect our soul and struggle to thrive.

Ideas only have power over us when we believe them. So, the question is, whose mental maps do you navigate reality by? Whose ideas do you trust in? Who do you put your faith in?

DISCUSS

As you consider what you just watched, use the following
questions to discuss these ideas, their basis in Scripture, and
their application in your life with your group members.

1 How often—daily, weekly, occasionally, rarely—do you have
unwanted, negative, harmful thoughts pop up in your mind?
How do you usually handle them?

2 How does Jesus' regard for the devil and his lies influence
the way you consider him as your enemy? How does it
change the way you see the devil and his attacks on you?

3 How does Jesus' warning about the enemy and his purpose—to steal, kill, destroy—make you feel? Afraid? Angry?
Concerned? Relieved? Something else? Explain.

4 Do you agree that your primary war with the devil requires you to believe truth over lies? How do you know what is true as you fight this spiritual battle?

5 How have the enemy's lies, perhaps during your childhood and upbringing, negatively followed you into adulthood? What lies about yourself do you struggle to dispel?

6 How has your faith in God influenced your ability to recognize the enemy's lies? What are some changes you have made in order to live in truth rather than lies?

LEARN

Pair up with another person in your group and briefly discuss how you are processing the ideas and information from this session. Be honest in how you're dealing with what you believe about the devil and his ability to attack you with lies. Focus your exchange with your partner around the following two questions:

- What concerns or troubles you the most so far? Why does it bother you? How are you handling it?
- What encourages and empowers you about what you've been learning and processing? Why?

After sharing your answers, commit to praying for your partner's concerns and ask him or her to do the same for you. If you're willing, exchange contact information so you can check in at least once between this meeting and the group's next session.

PRAY

Conclude this second session by reconvening with the group and sharing any prayer requests. Take a few minutes to pray together and thank God for all that you are discovering about his truth. Ask him to give each of you clarity, wisdom, and discernment about what is true and what is a lie within your thoughts, perceptions, and assumptions. Trust him to help you see clearly and to identify the lies of the devil woven into your daily struggles. Finally, thank God that his power and protection will guard you as you counter the enemy's lies with divine truth.

PERSONAL STUDY

Take some time to reflect on the material you've covered this week by engaging in any or all of the following between-sessions activities. Remember, these exercises are not intended to be homework or another obligation in your busy week but are simply provided to help you process what you've been thinking and feeling since your last group time. At the start of the next session, you will have a few minutes to share any insights you learned.

REFLECT

In this session, we saw how Jesus exposed Satan as "a murderer from the beginning" and said that "when he lies, he speaks his native language, for he is a liar and the father of lies" (John 8:44). By exposing Satan in this way, Jesus also revealed his identity as a life-giving Savior whose divine language is truth. Christ's words remind us that one of the best ways to counter the devil's lies is by focusing on God's truth. In the following passage, the apostle Paul reinforced this practice, reminding his readers to focus on what is true, life-giving, and holy rather than on the falsehoods and deceptive lies of the enemy:

> Rejoice in the Lord always. I will say it again: Rejoice! Let your gentleness be evident to all. The Lord is near. Do not be anxious about anything, but in every situation, by prayer and petition, with thanksgiving, present your requests to God. And the peace of God, which transcends all understanding, will guard your hearts and your minds in Christ Jesus.
>
> Finally, brothers and sisters, whatever is true, whatever is noble, whatever is right, whatever is pure, whatever is lovely, whatever is admirable—if anything is excellent or praiseworthy—think about such things. Whatever you have learned or received or heard from me, or seen in me—put it into practice. And the God of peace will be with you.
>
> *Philippians 4:4–9*

Why are you able to rejoice always, even in the midst of challenging circumstances? How does praying, giving thanks, and presenting your requests to God alleviate anxiety?

When in your life have you experienced "the peace of God, which transcends all understanding"? What were the circumstances?

How does focusing on that which is lovely, excellent, and praiseworthy eradicate the lies of the enemy from your thinking?

RECOGNIZE AND RESIST

Identifying the devil's lies and countering them with God's truth takes practice on our part and ongoing vigilance. It requires us to follow the apostle Paul's instruction to focus on those things that reflect God's love and the truth of Christ—those things that are true, noble, right, pure, lovely, admirable, excellent, and praiseworthy. But these qualities can seem abstract, and you may have different ideas about what they look like in your life as compared to someone else's. So, today take some time to complete the following exercises to make them more concrete. Read through the following questions, each grouped around the qualities listed in Philippians, and answer them as a way of equipping yourself with truth in order to dispel the lies of the enemy.

Whatever is true . .

Truth is measured by what God says in his Word. On a scale of 1 to 10—with 1 being "not sure" and 10 being "completely sure"— how confident are you that you know God's truth? What is the basis for the score you gave?

What is one truth from Scripture that has proved to be a good focal point for you? How can you focus on this truth in the course of your daily life?

Whatever is noble . . .

The word *noble* can be associated with royalty but it also means dignified, elevated, and beyond reproach. With this in mind, what does it mean to be elevated or dignified in your thoughts?

What are some lies that the enemy has tried to use lately to cause your thoughts to be anything less than "beyond reproach"? What types of thoughts tend to pull you away from trusting in Christ?

Whatever is right . . .

The word *right,* in this content, refers to something that conforms to custom or law. Much is said these days about discovering "what's right for you," but the Bible is clear that God has a *standard* of right living that he wants us to attain. Given this, how do you discern between what's right and wrong in today's "anything goes" culture?

Do you consider the Bible to be the source of what is definitively right and wrong? How do you regard the Bible and its guidelines about how you are to live in order to follow Jesus' example and please God?

Whatever is pure ...

Depending on your past experiences, the word *pure* may trigger feelings of guilt and shame. Knowing that you have made some mistakes—as everyone has—what does it mean for you to focus on what is pure?

Purity also implies wholeness. How does focusing on what is pure keep you whole? How does it help you counter the devil's lies that try to divide your thoughts and leave you fragmented in your resolve?

Whatever is lovely . . .

The word *lovely* refers not just to those things that are ascetically beautiful but also to those things that are pleasing and agreeable. What is the value in focusing your thoughts on what is "agreeable" in every situation? How would it help you in your interactions with others when things get tense?

As an adverb, *lovely* reminds us that the action was done "with love." What actions have others done for you lately that demonstrate their love and compassion? How have you shown lovely behavior to those around you?

Whatever is admirable . . .

The word *admirable* refers to traits or characteristics in others that you respect, appreciate, and admire. Who are the people you admire most in your life? What do you specifically admire about them?

What does it mean to be admirable in your words and actions toward others? How are you seeking to be more admirable in your interactions?

If anything is excellent . . .

Excellence is a word that is thrown around frequently today, often by advertisers and coaches, but it simply refers to having a virtuous character. In Paul's day, the word was used to describe those whose moral uprightness contributed to the welfare of society. What does excellence mean to you?

How can you think and act with excellence in your life? What changes in your current thinking would this require you to implement?

If anything is praiseworthy ...

The word *praiseworthy*, in this context, refers to those things that will bring commendation from God. What are some things in your life that you feel are especially praiseworthy in this sense? Why those traits?

Giving praise where praise is due is another way to define this final trait in the passage from Philippians. Who deserves praise in your life? How do these individuals reflect something of God's character and Jesus' example?

REJOICE

Paul advised the Philippians to not only focus their thoughts on what is true, noble, right, pure, lovely, admirable, excellent, and praiseworthy, but to also "rejoice in the Lord always." In fact, he felt so strongly about the point that he repeated the command: "I will say it again: Rejoice!" (Philippians 4:4). Consider this instruction as you answer the following questions.

What are you especially grateful for right now in your life?

What does it look like to rejoice in all things?

As you consider what you've learned in this study so far, what stands out the most? Do you feel there is a reason that you are studying these ideas on Satan's lies and God's truth at this particular time in your life? Explain.

At the end of your last group session, you traded contact information with a person in your group so that you could reach out to one another at least once before your next meeting. If you haven't connected yet, now is the time to reach out. This doesn't need to be formal or complicated—just send a text or give the person a call to touch base. Compare notes and see what is standing out for him or her from your group's last session. Write down a few key insights or any prayer requests from your discussion in the space below.

For Next Week: Before your group's next session, read chapters 5–8 in *Live No Lies*.

THE SLAVERY
OF FREEDOM

Those who are in the realm of
the flesh cannot please God.
ROMANS 8:8

WELCOME

Many of us think of the *flesh* as involving only lust, gluttony, or greed. But the truth is that each of us experiences all kinds of desires each day that pull us toward "the flesh." Whether it's a quest for more personal time away from our demands and responsibilities, or the latest luxury SUV, or a bowl of sugary cereal before bedtime, our hearts are continuously overflowing with desires and longings that compete with each other even as they contradict one another.

Perhaps you can relate. You feel the pull of being a good employee who does the job to the best of your ability . . . but you also feel the pull of taking it easy a bit and sliding by. You want to practice a healthy lifestyle that includes regular exercise, eating the right food, and getting enough uninterrupted sleep at night . . . but you also feel the pull of instead lounging on the couch, eating unhealthy food that tastes good, and staying up late. You like to think of yourself as a good steward of all the blessings and resources you've been given . . . but you also feel the pull of splurging on designer purses or the latest tech gadgetry.

It's likely that you've found this struggle is especially apparent in your faith and relationship with Christ. Sure, you want to get up early enough to spend time with God before you have to head out to work . . . but you also want to get just a bit more sleep. You want to actively participate in your local church and serve others . . . but you only have so much time! It's much easier to skip the church services and let others do the volunteering.

Even as your heart wrestles with these competing desires, the culture at large is telling you to just be true to yourself, live out your own truth, reject the agendas of others, and follow your heart. Much of Western culture perpetuates the idea that your internal desires are the best roadmap to living "the good life" and that you should always get what you want because, you know, *you deserve it.* But God's Word says that living in this manner leads to death (see Romans 8:6).

It is a serious problem that we face . . . and one that certainly can't be ignored. So, what is the solution? How will we win this war against the enemy of the flesh? As we will discuss in this session, the victory comes in following this command from Christ: "Whoever wants to be my disciple must deny themselves and take up their cross and follow me. For whoever wants to save their life will lose it, but whoever loses their life for me will find it" (Matthew 16:24–25).

SHARE

Take a few minutes to share any insights you have from last week's personal study. Then, to get things started, discuss one of the following questions:

- What indulgence, splurge, or guilty pleasure often causes you to give in to temptation? Mindless television? Impulse snack purchases? Something else?

— *or* —

- What is one regular habit or personal discipline you maintain no matter what? Exercising every day? Flossing and brushing? Unplugging before bed?

READ

Invite someone to read aloud the following passage. Listen for fresh insights as you hear the verse being read and then discuss the questions that follow.

As for you, you were dead in your transgressions and sins, in which you used to live when you followed the ways of this world and of the ruler of the kingdom of the air, the spirit who is now at work in those who are disobedient. All of us also lived among them at one time, gratifying the cravings of our flesh and following its desires and thoughts. Like the rest, we were by nature deserving of wrath. But because of his great love for us, God, who is rich in mercy, made us alive with Christ even when we were dead in transgressions—it is by grace you have been saved. And God raised us up with Christ and seated us with him in the heavenly realms in Christ Jesus, in order that in the coming ages he might show the incomparable riches of his grace, expressed in his kindness to us in Christ Jesus. For it is by grace you have been saved, through faith—and this is not from yourselves, it is the gift of God—not by works, so that no one can boast. For

we are God's handiwork, created in Christ Jesus to do
good works, which God prepared in advance for us to do.

Ephesians 2:1–10

What comes to mind when you consider "the cravings of our
flesh"? How does Paul describe your condition when you were
ruled by the flesh?

Based on this passage, what is the reason that you are able to
overcome the enemy of the flesh? What does Paul say is your
condition now?

WATCH

Play the video segment for session three (see the streaming video access provided on the inside front cover). As you watch, use the following outline to record any thoughts or concepts that stand out to you.

Martin Luther King, Jr. said, "Inside all of us, there is a civil war raging on the battlefield of our desire." The human heart is beautiful, mysterious, and full of desires that are complex and often contradictory.

Some of our desires are good and lead to life, peace, freedom, and God's true nature. They are God's desires in our own desires. But other desires are evil and base and lead to compulsion, full-on addiction, fear, and even death.

The word Paul and other writers of the New Testament used for this aspect of our inner desires is the *flesh*. The flesh represents our base, primal, animalistic drive for self-gratification—especially pertaining to sensuality, but also to pleasure and our instincts for survival, domination, and the need for control.

If we go deep enough, we find the ache is for God—to live in his love, yield to his gentle peace, let our bodies become a place where his will is done on earth as it is in heaven, and become a person of love just like Jesus was.

The "self" that Jesus is calling us to deny and put to death isn't our authentic self before God. It's our *flesh*, which is actually keeping us from actualizing our true self in God. The more we give in to the cultural messaging to follow our heart, the more we devolve to the lowest common denominator.

The solution to the problem of the flesh is not *willpower* but the *Spirit's* power. It's habituating your heart into obedience to Jesus through practices that enable you to yield and surrender all of your heart over to God.

DISCUSS

As you consider what you just watched, use the following
questions to discuss these ideas, their basis in Scripture, and
their application in your life with your group members.

1 On a daily basis, how aware are you of the competing
desires within yourself? Can you share a recent example,
keeping it appropriate for your group setting?

2 How would you define or describe the biblical concept of
"the flesh" that Paul and other New Testament writers iden-
tified within the human heart?

3 Do you agree that all people have deeper and truer longings
than the ones front-and-center in their consciousness? Why
or why not?

4 How does getting in touch with your longing to know God and follow Jesus help you to overcome temptations of the flesh? How do you handle your emotions when you're being tempted by something your flesh really wants?

5 What are some examples from popular culture you've seen that encourage you to do whatever makes you happy? How do you typically deal with these messages?

6 How has cultivating your spiritual life helped you to change destructive habits and selfish desires? Again, can you share an example that's appropriate for your group?

LEARN

Learning to identify your competing desires may sound easy. But it requires intentional awareness on your part to guard against the devil's lies and the rationalizations that he creates to compel you to follow the flesh. So, for this closing activity, you will make a list to identify some of the desires that might be operating in your heart right now. Note this is a private list, for your eyes only, unless you decide to share it with others. The key is to be honest with yourself as you look into your heart and try to discern what your spirit wants and what your flesh wants.

Desires related to how you spend your time

Spirit Desires

_____

_____

_____

Flesh Desires

_____

_____

_____

Examples

_____

_____

_____

Examples

_____

_____

_____

Desires related to your primary relationships

Spirit Desires

_____

_____

_____

Flesh Desires

_____

_____

_____

Examples   *Examples*

_____   _____

_____   _____

_____   _____

Desires related to how you use your money

Spirit Desires   *Flesh Desires*

_____   _____

_____   _____

_____   _____

Examples   *Examples*

_____   _____

_____   _____

_____   _____

Desires related to what you enjoy the most

Spirit Desires   *Flesh Desires*

_____   _____

_____   _____

_____   _____

Examples   *Examples*

_____   _____

_____   _____

_____   _____

Other desires

Spirit Desires   *Flesh Desires*

_____   _____

_____   _____

_____   _____

Examples   *Examples*

_____   _____

_____   _____

_____   _____

PRAY

Conclude your session by sharing any requests you would like the group to lift up in prayer, especially as they relate to the exercise you just completed. As you pray for one another, ask God to protect you and empower you against the lies of the devil and the desires of your flesh. Thank him for the gift of grace that frees you from the burden of living only according to your fleshly desires. Praise him for sending Jesus to set you free so that you can experience spiritual freedom and live in the truth—not the lies of enemies.

PERSONAL STUDY

Take some time to reflect on the material you've covered this week by engaging in any or all of the following between-sessions activities. Remember, these exercises are not intended to be homework or another obligation in your busy week but are simply provided to help you process what you've been thinking and feeling since your last group time. At the start of the next session, you will have a few minutes to share any insights you learned.

REFLECT

One of the best ways to become more aware of what's going on in your heart—both the desires of your spirit as well as your flesh—is to spend some quiet time alone before God. As simple as this sounds, in our 24/7-always-online world, unplugging and disconnecting from the distractions, demands, and disruptions of life can be challenging. Like any other spiritual discipline that you do to draw you closer to God, it requires regular practice.

So today, set your smartphone, watch, or other device for five minutes (or ten if you're feeling daring) and silence all texts, calls, emails, noises, and vibrations. Find a comfortable place where you can sit without anyone else disturbing you. Take a few deep breaths, set the timer, and close your eyes if you want. Once the time has passed, answer the questions below to help you become more aware of how God is at work in the desires of your heart.

What thoughts passed through your mind just now? Did you get to a point when you felt more at peace and quiet within your spirit? Explain.

Did you gravitate toward a particular idea, image, word, or phrase during this time? What relevance does it have in your life right now?

What desires surfaced during this time of reflection? Other than perhaps wanting the exercise to be over, what were you aware of wanting as you reached a place of quiet stillness within?

RECOGNIZE AND RESIST

Each of us, at times, is guilty of doing things that we know are not good for us in the long-term but provide pleasure, relief, comfort, or escape in the short-term. It might be grabbing a couple donuts before work, buying things you know you cannot afford, bingeing on video games, or gambling on sports teams. While some of these habits may have started as benign coping mechanisms, anything we turn to instead of God can quickly become an idol.

In the Bible, God tells his people that he is "a jealous God" and that they are to have "no other gods" before him (Exodus 20:5, 3). He makes this warning not to be punitive but because he knows that pursuit of anything other than him will not lead to fulfillment in life. God created us and knows what we need in order to thrive even better than we know ourselves. So, when he issues these commands in Scripture to put no other gods before him, it is for our own good.

Of course, even when you want to put God first, you can find yourself falling back into old habits, thought patterns, and addictive behaviors. Breaking out of these ways of coping requires a clear understanding of what is true—about God, about who he made you to be, and what his purpose is for your life. The apostle Paul understood this dilemma firsthand and expressed his frustration in the following passage to the believers in Rome. Read through these verses, underline any words or phrases that express your own experience and feelings about the battle between your fleshly desires and your spirit, and then answer the questions that follow.

I do not understand what I do. For what I want to do I do not do, but what I hate I do. And if I do what I do not want to do, I agree that the law is good. As it is, it is no longer I myself who do it, but it is sin living in me. For I know that good itself does not dwell in me, that is, in my sinful nature. For I have the desire to do what is good, but I cannot carry it out. For I do not do the good I want to do, but the evil I do not want to do—this I keep on doing. Now if I do what I do not want to do, it is no longer I who do it, but it is sin living in me that does it.

So I find this law at work: Although I want to do good, evil is right there with me. For in my inner being I delight in God's law; but I see another law at work in me, waging war against the law of my mind and making me a prisoner of the law of sin at work within me. What a wretched man I am! Who will rescue me from this body that is subject to death? Thanks be to God, who delivers me through Jesus Christ our Lord!

Romans 7:15–25

Go back and look at the words and phrases you underlined. How do they reflect what is in your heart right now?

How do those words and phrases you underlined express your frustration over past mistakes and present temptations?

Do you agree with Paul that you cannot save yourself from this war that is raging within? Why or why not?

How has your life changed since you first started following Jesus? What habits and behaviors have you given up? Which new ones have you added?

What do you do now when you stumble and give in to temptation? Has your response changed over time? If so, how has it changed?

How has inviting Jesus into your life delivered you from the slavery of your own desires? How has God's grace and truth set you free?

REJOICE

You can sometimes feel alone when you choose to go against the conventional wisdom of the world and live in God's truth instead of the enemy's lies. In fact, the devil would love nothing more than to play off this sense of loneliness. *No one else is making sacrifices—they're enjoying themselves! God just wants to spoil your fun and take the pleasure out of life. It won't really matter if you cave on your morals a bit and give in this time.* On and on it goes.

But the truth is that you are never as isolated as the enemy would lead you to believe. In the Old Testament, we read how the prophet Elijah once despaired that he was the only one in all of Israel who was still faithfully following the Lord. He said to God, "The Israelites have rejected your covenant, torn down your altars, and put your prophets to death with the sword. I am the only one left." But the Lord had this reply to Elijah's claim: "I reserve seven thousand in Israel—all whose knees have not bowed down to Baal" (1 Kings 19:10, 18).

God made us to be social beings who require relationships in order to grow. So, throughout the Bible, we are urged to support and encourage one another and help each other as we go forward together in life. The depth and strength of our faith, according to Scripture, relies on how we both give and receive spiritual encouragement to and from those around us:

> Let us hold unswervingly to the hope we profess, for he who promised is faithful. And let us consider how we may spur one another on toward love and good deeds, not giving up meeting together, as some are in the habit of doing, but encouraging one another—and all the more as you see the Day approaching.
>
> *Hebrews 10:23–25*

With this in mind, contact someone from your group to check in and see how he or she is doing. Listen for ways you can encourage that person and assist him or her in recognizing the enemy's lies. Write down a few reflections in the space below after you connect with the person.

For Next Week: Before your group's next session, read chapters 9–10 and the epilogue in *Live No Lies*.

THE REALITY ABOUT NORMALITY

Do not love the world or
anything in the world.
1 JOHN 2:15

WELCOME

Go with the flow. Don't rock the boat. Do whatever it takes to fit in. Be part of the team. Just do what everyone else is doing. These are the lies that the world, the third enemy of our souls, attempts to get us to believe. If the devil is the source of evil, and the flesh is our own sinful proclivity for following our own desires, then the world is the melting pot where the two meet.

In the New Testament, the term *world* can refer to our planet (see Acts 17:24) or to the inhabitants of our world (see John 1:10). But it can also refer to something more sinister—a system of practices in our society based on secularism, humanism, and hedonism. It is this type of system that Jesus had in mind when he warned his followers, "If the world hates you, keep in mind that it hated me first. If you belonged to the world, it would love you as its own. As it is, you do not belong to the world, but I have chosen you out of the world" (John 15:18–19).

Christ's words reflect the dilemma that all believers face today. We are human, living in time and space on this planet, but we are not to take part in the world's spirit, values, or habits. We are to remember that "our citizenship is in heaven" (Philippians 3:20) and that we are "children of God . . . [not] under the control of the evil one" (1 John 5:19).

We are to remember that we "are not in the realm of the flesh but are in the realm of the Spirit" (Romans 8:9). For this reason, as believers in God's truth, we should not "conform to the pattern of this world" (Romans 12:2).

We find all this instruction in the Bible to live apart from the world . . . and yet the fact remains that we live in this world and are not immune to its influence and charms. So, what is the answer? How is it possible to live *in* the world but not be *part* of it? As we will discuss in this final session, the answer lies in tapping into the power of the Holy Spirit—and it also lies in connecting with other likeminded believers who are intent on staying separate from the world.

SHARE

Take a few minutes to share any insights you have from last week's personal study. Then, to get things started, discuss one of the following questions:

- What's something you do that you consider "normal," such as a habit or behavior, that others have informed you is rather unique and not normal at all?

— *or* —

- When have you recently joined in with what the majority wanted or the group was doing? Were you aware you were caving to peer pressure at the time?

READ

Invite someone to read aloud the following passage. Listen for fresh insights as you hear the verse being read and then discuss the questions that follow.

"I am coming to you now, but I say these things while I am still in the world, so that they may have the full measure of my joy within them. I have given them your word and the world has hated them, for they are not of the world any more than I am of the world. My prayer is not that you take them out of the world but that you protect them from the evil one. They are not of the world, even as I am not of it. Sanctify them by the truth; your word is truth. As you sent me into the world, I have sent them into the world. For them I sanctify myself, that they too may be truly sanctified."

John 17:13–19

Why do you think Jesus prayed this prayer the night before his death on the cross? What does the timing tell you about what he considered urgent to bring before his heavenly Father?

How do you believe the truth of Christ protects you from the lies of this world? When have you experienced this kind of protection?

WATCH

Play the video segment for session four (see the streaming video access provided on the inside front cover). As you watch, use the following outline to record any thoughts or concepts that stand out to you.

The word *cosmos* in the Greek has a few different meanings in the New Testament. Sometimes it just means planet Earth. Other times it means humanity. But it can also refer to something darker and more sinister—a system of practices and standards associated with secular society.

The *world* can thus be defined as a system of ideas, values, morals, practices, and social norms that are integrated into the mainstream and eventually institutionalized in a culture that is corrupted by the twin sins of rebellion against God and the redefinition of good and evil.

In the world, especially in the secular west, we no longer get our bearings at a moral level from God. The new authority is the self, defined as our desires and our feelings. As a result, we've completely lost a sense of direction other than our own emotional rudder, which all too frequently leads us astray.

We are far more socially influenced creatures than we want to believe. Behaviors, good or bad, spread through networks of family, friends, neighborhoods, and cities in a similar way to a virus or contagious disease that's airborne.

We were created by a relational God to live in relationship. But under the Fall, we devolve back into tribal pack animals. This is often how the devil's deceptive ideas keep such a strong hold on societies and souls for so very long.

Surrender your autonomy to love. Place yourself in the constraint of community, for it is there that you will be set free from your flesh. Give up your preferences for the sake of others. Enroll in the school of *agape* with teacher Jesus.

DISCUSS

As you consider what you just watched, use the following questions to discuss these ideas, their basis in Scripture, and their application in your life with your group members.

1 How would you define "the world" as an enemy of your soul? How does the world work with the devil and the flesh to steal your peace and undermine your wholeness?

2 What are some ways you have set yourself apart from the world in your lifestyle choices? How do these methods keep you anchored in truth and aware of the world's lies?

3   What does it mean to be *in* the world but not *of* the world? How would you describe this distinctive to someone who is new to faith in Christ?

4   What are some examples of ways the world and its customs, beliefs, and values have shifted in your lifetime? What has surprised you the most in what you have witnessed? What continues to trouble you?

5   How do you find yourself subtly conforming to the lies of the world? How do you combat these lies and temptations?

6   What is the role of the church in helping its members to overcome the lies of the world? How has this small group served that purpose during these four sessions?

LEARN

As this study wraps up, it is important for you to continue supporting one another and encouraging each other as you seek to follow the truth of Christ. Toward that goal, get in pairs or triads, read the following passage together, and then spend a few minutes comparing your answers to the questions that follow.

> For though we live in the world, we do not wage war as the world does. The weapons we fight with are not the weapons of the world. On the contrary, they have divine power to demolish strongholds. We demolish arguments and every pretension that sets itself up against the knowledge of God, and we take captive every thought to make it obedient to Christ. And we will be ready to punish every act of disobedience, once your obedience is complete.
>
> *2 Corinthians 10:3–6*

What are the spiritual resources you rely on the most to overcome the spiritual war for your soul? Why do you find those resources valuable?

How do you "demolish arguments and every pretension that sets itself up against the knowledge of God" in your daily life? How do you do this in a way that honors Christ and reflects the love of God?

How can others support you as this group concludes and you continue to fight the good fight and grow in your faith?

PRAY

Conclude this final session by going around the room and allowing everyone to share: (1) what they are especially thankful for from this group, (2) a current personal prayer request that they would like answered, and (3) an ongoing need for prayer to help them continue to win the battle. Follow this with a time of thanking and praising God for the victory you have through the truth of Jesus and the power of God's Word. Lift up one another's needs and requests as the Holy Spirit leads you. Then ask God to protect you from the enemy and to help you see through his lies. Ask for strength and perseverance as you become aware of the ways your flesh continues to try and pull you away from what your spirit wants. Finally, ask for wisdom and discernment on how to live in this world without conforming to its depravity and secularism.

PERSONAL STUDY

Take some time to reflect on the material you've covered this final week by engaging in any or all of the following between-sessions activities. Remember, these exercises are not intended to be homework or another obligation in your busy week but are provided to help you process what you've been thinking and feeling since your last group time. In this final time of reflection, you may also want to review your previous answers, either going back to previous personal studies in this guide or referring to the journal or notebook you used for your responses. In the coming days, be sure to share any insights you learned with one of your fellow group members.

REFLECT

Perhaps one of Jesus' best-known sayings about the world is a warning to his followers not to fall under its spell: "What good will it be for someone to gain the whole world, yet forfeit their soul?" (Matthew 16:26). Jesus understood the lure of the world system and the pull it has over human beings. Yet Jesus also saw the world as an actual *threat* that his followers needed to guard against: "If the world hates you, keep in mind that it hated me first. . . . If they persecuted me, they will persecute you also" (John 15:18, 20). Just as the world would eventually crucify him, so the world would treat them in a similar manner. The relationship is hostile.

Given this reality, we might expect Jesus to instruct his followers to completely withdraw from the world and exist in isolated communities—and, in fact, we find that many early believers followed this course. Yet the truth is that Jesus never instructed his followers to take such action. Rather, we find him making requests like these to his heavenly Father: "My prayer is not that you take them out of the world but that you protect them from the evil one" (John 17:15).

So, why wouldn't Jesus ask the Father to take his children out of this world—especially since he knew they would suffer persecution? The following passages, which took place after Jesus' resurrection and right before his ascension into heaven, provide a few clues on his intent. Read through each of these verses and then answer the questions that follow.

> Then the eleven disciples went to Galilee, to the mountain where Jesus had told them to go. When they saw him, they worshiped him; but some doubted. Then Jesus came to them and said, "All authority in heaven and on earth has been given to me. Therefore go and make disciples of all nations, baptizing them in the name of the Father and of the Son and of the Holy Spirit, and teaching them to obey everything I have commanded you. And surely I am with you always, to the very end of the age."
>
> *Matthew 28:16–20*

Then they gathered around him and asked him, "Lord, are you at this time going to restore the kingdom to Israel?" He said to them: "It is not for you to know the times or dates the Father has set by his own authority. But you will receive power when the Holy Spirit comes on you; and you will be my witnesses in Jerusalem, and in all Judea and Samaria, and to the ends of the earth."

Acts 1:6–8

What command did Jesus give his followers in Matthew 28:16–20? What promise did he make to them as they remained in this world?

What did Jesus say would happen to his followers in Acts 1:6–8? What were they to do when this came to pass?

Paul would later write that we are "Christ's ambassadors" (2 Corinthians 5:20). How did Jesus see his followers as his ambassadors to this world?

RECOGNIZE AND RESIST

Throughout the centuries, followers of Jesus have accepted this "great commission" to spread the message of the gospel to a lost and hurting world. They have chosen to remain in the world and engaged in society so they could be effective ambassadors of God's love. We see this clearly in the life of the apostle Paul, who wrote, "I have become all things to all people so that by all possible means I might save some" (1 Corinthians 9:22). Still, living in the world comes with the threat of being enticed by the world's system. There is constant pressure to compromise our values and become "lukewarm" in our faith. This was a problem that Jesus pointed out to one early group of believers in the book of Revelation, as the following passage relates.

"To the angel of the church in Laodicea write:
      These are the words of the Amen, the faithful and true witness, the ruler of God's creation. I know your

deeds, that you are neither cold nor hot. I wish you were either one or the other! So, because you are lukewarm—neither hot nor cold—I am about to spit you out of my mouth. You say, 'I am rich; I have acquired wealth and do not need a thing.' But you do not realize that you are wretched, pitiful, poor, blind and naked. I counsel you to buy from me gold refined in the fire, so you can become rich; and white clothes to wear, so you can cover your shameful nakedness; and salve to put on your eyes, so you can see.

Those whom I love I rebuke and discipline. So be earnest and repent. Here I am! I stand at the door and knock. If anyone hears my voice and opens the door, I will come in and eat with that person, and they with me.

To the one who is victorious, I will give the right to sit with me on my throne, just as I was victorious and sat down with my Father on his throne. Whoever has ears, let them hear what the Spirit says to the churches."

Revelation 3:14–22

What was Jesus' complaint against this church? How is it evident from his words that they were not separating themselves from the ways of the world?

What were these believers failing to recognize about their "luke-warm" state?

What did Christ command them to do to change their ways?

What promise does Jesus make to them if they choose to obey his commands?

What does this say about the dangers of allowing yourself to be conformed to the world?

What is one area in your life in which you have been conforming to the world? What will you do today to submit that area to Jesus' authority?

Review your notes, questions, and reflections you jotted down while watching the video teaching as well as anything else you noted during and after each group session. Think about where you were spiritually then and where you see yourself now. Then use the following questions to help you evaluate and summarize your overall experience.

What stands our as you look back through your notes? Are there consistent themes you see running throughout all your experiences?

How has your view of Jesus changed over the course of meeting with your group? How has the way you see yourself changed? Where do you see evidence of this change in your notes, answers, and written reflections?

How has your awareness of the spiritual war in which you are engaged changed since you started this study? What have you learned about defeating the three enemies of your soul that was not clear to you before?

What particular passages and verses from God's Word have empowered you as you've battled the lies of your enemies? Which specific truths from the Bible are especially significant to you at this time? Why?

REJOICE

Close out this study by making a few notes about the truths you have discovered that continue to resonate in your heart. Think about each group member and consider how he or she contributed to your overall experience. Use this final set of questions to help you bring closure to your study and carry your experiences with you in the days and weeks ahead.

What are some of the specific moments, people, and events from your group's meetings for which you're particularly thankful?

What surprised you the most about your group experience? What disappointed you or left you frustrated?

What is one key lesson that you learned about the *devil*?

What is one key lesson that you learned about the *flesh*?

What is one key lesson that you learned about the *world*?

What will you carry with you now that your group has concluded? How have you changed the most since starting and completing these sessions?

Finally, decide on how you will continue to love, support, and encourage your fellow members. Before more than a week or two have passed, choose at least one other group member and send him or her a text or email to see how things are going now that the group has concluded. When you connect with that person, ask who he or she chose to reach out to from your group. Try to make sure that everyone in your group hears from someone else. If the group wants to continue meeting, make a plan for your next study. Or, if the group disbands, continue checking on the friends you made and asking how you can pray for them.

LEADER'S GUIDE

Thank you for your willingness to lead a small group through this study. What you have chosen to do is valuable and will make a great difference in the lives of others. The rewards of being a leader are different from those of participating, and we hope that as you lead you will find your own walk with Jesus deepened by the experience.

Live No Lies is a four-session Bible study built around video content and small-group interaction. As the group leader, imagine yourself as the host of a party. Your job is to take care of your guests by managing the behind-the-scenes details so that as your guests arrive, they can focus on one another and on the interaction around the topic for that week.

Your role as the group leader is not to answer all the questions or reteach the content—the video, book, and study guide will do most of that work. Your job is to guide the experience and cultivate your small group into a connected and engaged community. This will make it a place for members to process, question, and reflect—not necessarily receive more instruction.

There are several elements in this leader's guide that will help you as you structure your study and reflection time, so be sure to follow along and take advantage of each one.

BEFORE YOU BEGIN

Before your first meeting, make sure the group members have a copy of this study guide. Alternately, you can hand out the study guides at your first meeting and give the members some time to look over the material and ask any preliminary questions. Also make sure they are aware that they have access to the videos at any time through the streaming code provided on the inside front cover. During your first meeting, send a sheet of paper around the room and have the members write down their name, phone number, and email address so you can keep in touch with them during the week.

Generally, the ideal size for a group is eight to ten people, which will ensure that everyone has enough time to participate in discussions. If you have more people, you might want to break up the main group into smaller subgroups. Encourage those who show up at the first meeting to commit to attending the duration of the study, as this will help the group members get to know one another, create stability for the group, and help you know how to best prepare each week.

Each of the sessions begins with an opening reflection. The questions that follow in the "Share" section serve as an icebreaker to get the group members thinking about the general topic at hand. Some people may want to tell a long story in response to one of these questions, but the goal is to keep the answers brief. Ideally, you want everyone in the group to get a chance to answer, so try to keep the responses to a minute or less. If you have talkative group members, say up front that everyone needs to limit their answer to one minute.

Give the group members a chance to answer, but also tell them to feel free to pass if they wish. With the rest of the study, it's generally not a good idea to have everyone answer every question—a free-flowing discussion is more desirable. But with the opening icebreaker-type questions, you can go around the circle. Encourage shy people to share, but don't force them.

At your first meeting, let the group members know each session contains a personal study section that they can use to reflect more on the content during the week. While this is an optional exercise, it will help the members cement the concepts presented during the group study time and encourage them to spend time each day in God's Word. Let them know that if they choose to do so, they can watch the video for the following week by accessing the streaming code found on the inside front cover of their studies. Invite them to bring any questions and insights they uncovered while reading to your next meeting, especially if they had a breakthrough moment or didn't understand something.

WEEKLY PREPARATION

As the leader, there are a few things you should do to prepare for each meeting:

- *Read through the session.* This will help you to become more familiar with the content and know how to structure the discussion times.
- *Decide how the videos will be used.* Determine whether you want the members to watch the videos ahead of time (via the streaming access code found on the inside front cover) or together as a group.
- *Decide which questions you want to discuss.* Based on the amount and length of group discussion, you may not be able to get through all the questions, so choose four to five that you definitely want to cover.
- *Be familiar with the questions you want to discuss.* When the group meets, you'll be watching the clock, so you want to make sure you are familiar with the questions you have selected. In this way, you'll ensure you have the material more deeply in your mind than your group members.
- *Pray for your group.* Pray for your group members throughout the week and ask God to lead them as they study his Word.

In many cases, there will be no one "right" answer to the question. Answers will vary, especially when the group members are being asked to share their personal experiences.

STRUCTURING THE DISCUSSION TIME

You will need to determine with your group how long you want to meet each week so you can plan your time accordingly. Generally, most groups like to meet for either ninety minutes or two hours, so you could use one of the following schedules:

SECTION	90 MINUTES	120 MINUTES
Welcome (members arrive and get settled)	10 minutes	15 minutes
Share (discuss one or more of the opening questions for the session)	10 minutes	15 minutes
Read (discuss the questions based on the Scripture reading for the week)	10 minutes	15 minutes
Watch (watch the teaching material together and take notes)	15 minutes	15 minutes
Discuss (discuss the Bible study questions you selected ahead of time)	25 minutes	35 minutes
Learn (go through the closing exercise)	10 minutes	15 minutes
Pray (pray as a group and dismiss)	10 minutes	10 minutes

As the group leader, it is up to you to keep track of the time and keep things on schedule. You might want to set a timer for each segment so both you and the group members know when your time is up. (There are some good phone apps for timers that play a gentle chime or other pleasant sound instead of a disruptive noise.)

Don't be concerned if the group members are quiet or slow to share. People are often quiet when they are pulling together their ideas, and this might be a new experience for them. Just ask a question and let it hang in the air until someone shares. You can then say, "Thank you. What about others? What came to you when you watched that portion of the teaching?"

GROUP DYNAMICS

Leading a group through *Live No Lies* will prove to be highly rewarding both to you and your group members. But you still may encounter challenges along the way! Discussions can get off track. Group members may not be sensitive to the needs and ideas of others. Some might worry they will be expected to talk about matters that make them feel awkward. Others may express comments that result in disagreements. To help ease this strain on you and the group, consider the following ground rules:

- When someone raises a question or comment that is off the main topic, suggest that you deal with it another time, or, if you feel led to go in that direction, let the group know you will be spending some time discussing it.
- If someone asks a question that you don't know how to answer, admit it and move on. At your discretion, feel free to invite group members to comment on questions that call for personal experience.
- If you find one or two people are dominating the discussion time, direct a few questions to others in the group. Outside the main group time, ask the more

dominating members to help you draw out the quieter ones. Work to make them a part of the solution instead of part of the problem.

- When a disagreement occurs, encourage the group members to process the matter in love. Encourage those on opposite sides to restate what they heard the other side say about the matter, and then invite each side to evaluate if that perception is accurate. Lead the group in examining other Scriptures related to the topic and look for common ground.

When any of these issues arise, encourage your group members to follow these words from the Bible: "Love one another" (John 13:34), "If it is possible, as far as it depends on you, live at peace with everyone" (Romans 12:18), "Whatever is true . . . noble . . . right . . . if anything is excellent or praiseworthy—think about such things" (Philippians 4:8), and "Be quick to listen, slow to speak and slow to become angry" (James 1:19). This will make your group time more rewarding and beneficial for everyone who attends.

Thank you again for taking the time to lead your group. You are making a difference in the lives of others and having an impact on the kingdom of God.

It's Not the Height
of the Giant
... but the Size of
Our God

Explore the principles in *Goliath Must Fall* with your small group through this six-session video-based study. Each week, pastor Louie Giglio will provide practical steps and biblical principles for how you and your group can defeat the "giants" in your lives like fear, rejection, comfort, anger, or addiction. Includes discussion questions, Bible exploration, and personal study materials for in between sessions.

Available now at your favorite bookstore,
or streaming video on StudyGateway.com.

Video Study for Your Church or Small Group

If you've enjoyed this book, now you can go deeper with the companion video Bible study!

In this six-session study, Louie Giglio helps you apply the principles in *Don't Give the Enemy a Seat at Your Table* to your life. The study guide includes video notes, group discussion questions, and personal study materials for in between sessions.

Study Guide
9780310134244

DVD with
Free Streaming Access
9780310134268

Available now at your favorite bookstore,
or streaming video on StudyGateway.com.

Also available from Jennie Allen

Available now at your favorite bookstore or
streaming video on StudyGateway.com

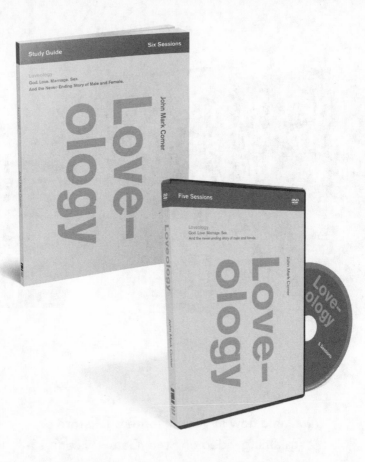